From:

x Jacobs x

Illustrations copyright © 1998 Jacqueline Mair
This edition copyright © 1998 Lion Publishing

Published by
**Lion Publishing plc**
Sandy Lane West, Oxford, England
ISBN 0 7459 3998 8

First edition 1998
10 9 8 7 6 5 4 3 2 1 0

A catalogue record for this book is available from the
British Library
Printed and bound in Singapore

## Acknowledgments

We would like to thank all those who have given us
permission to include material in this book. Every effort
has been made to trace and acknowledge copyright
holders of all the quotations included. We apologize for
any errors or omissions that may remain, and would ask
those concerned to contact the publishers, who will
ensure that full acknowledgment is made in the future.

All quotes by K. Bradford Brown © K. Bradford Brown,
published by Lifetimes Press.

Scriptures quoted from the *Good News Bible*
published by The Bible Societies/HarperCollins
Publishers Ltd, UK © American Bible Society, 1966,
1971, and 4th edition 1976.

♥ H E A R T F E L T S

# Best Friends

COMPILED BY FRANCES GRANT

LION
Publishing

# BEST FRIENDS

Having best friends, distant or near, sharing ourselves with others, with a strength and yet a lightness of touch, can bring a sense of real joy into our lives. The Bible teaches that the greatest gift of all is to give of ourselves in friendship.

♥

These treasured quotations enable us to honour our friends in a myriad of ways. In so doing, we may also discover our friendship with God.

♥

A life
without a friend
is a life
without
a sun.

GERMAN PROVERB

It is mutual
respect
which makes
friendship
lasting.

JOHN HENRY NEWMAN

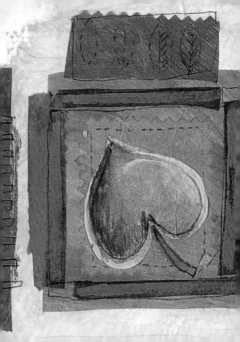

The thought came loud
and clear this morning:
the travelling *is* the
arriving, the way *is* the
achievement. I miss out
so much if all I wish for
my friendships is jam
tomorrow.

DOUGLAS GIFFORD

Two are better than one,
because together they can
work more effectively.
If one of them falls
down, the other one can
lift him up.

FROM THE OLD TESTAMENT
BOOK OF ECCLESIASTES

♥

When friendship is funny, and bright, we click. And then we need the *soft, quiet* times together, to make it real.

FRANCES GRANT

♥

Believe me, my young friend, there is nothing — absolutely nothing — half so much worth doing as simply messing about in boats.

KENNETH GRAHAME

Better by far
you should forget
and smile
Than that you
should
remember and
be sad.

CHRISTINA ROSSETTI

The essence of a
perfect friendship
is that each friend
reveals himself utterly
to the other, flings
aside his reserves,
and shows himself
for what he truly is.

ROBERT BENSON

But if the while I think on thee, dear friend, All losses are restor'd and sorrows end.

WILLIAM SHAKESPEARE

Friendships begun in
this world will
be taken up again,
never to be
broken off.

FRANCES DE SALES

True
friendship
ought never
to conceal
what it thinks.

ST JEROME

Accept one
    another, then...
as you
    yourself are
accepted in love.

FROM THE NEW TESTAMENT
BOOK OF ROMANS

Blessed is he who hungers for friends, for though he may not realize it, his soul is crying out for God.

HABIB SAHABIB

God evidently
does not
intend us all to
be rich or
powerful or
great;

but he does
intend us all to
be friends.

RALPH WALDO EMERSON

My spiritual friend

accepts me

as I am,

and empowers me

to be more than

I think I can be.

K. BRADFORD BROWN

If I had to choose
between betraying
my country and
betraying my
friend, I hope
I should have the
guts to betray my
country.

E.M. FORSTER

The impulse of love
that leads us to the
doorway of a friend is
the *voice of God within*,
and we need not be
afraid to follow it.

AGNES SANDFORD

A friendship
which makes
the least noise is
very often
the most useful;

♥

for which
reason I
should
prefer a prudent
friend to a
zealous one!

JOSEPH ADDISON

True friendship
is a plant of slow
growth, and must
undergo and
withstand the shocks
of adversity before it
is entitled to the
appellation.

GEORGE WASHINGTON

Friendship is not a fruit for enjoyment only, but also an opportunity for service.

GREEK PROVERB

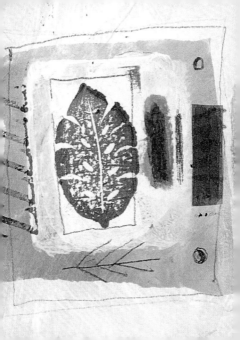

As a friend
one is a
person for
other people to rely
on. A friend remains
a friend,
even in disaster,
even in guilt.

JÜRGEN MOLTMANN

A judicious choice of friends is essential to happiness. The daily round of work is much more pleasant if cheered by friends who are often able to give, or pleased to receive, help in the little difficulties that occur in everyday life.

ISABELLA BEETON

I shall pass this way but once. Any good therefore that I can do, or any kindness that I can show to any human being, let me do it now, let me not defer it nor neglect it, for I shall not pass this way again.

UNKNOWN

The greatest
love a person

can have for his

friends is to give

his life for them.

FROM THE NEW TESTAMENT
GOSPEL OF JOHN

Every man should keep a fair-sized cemetery, in which to bury the faults of his friends.

HENRY WARD BEECHER

To know someone
here or there with
whom you feel there
is understanding in
spite of distances or
thoughts unexpressed
— that can make of
this earth a garden.

JOHANN WOLFGANG VON GOETHE

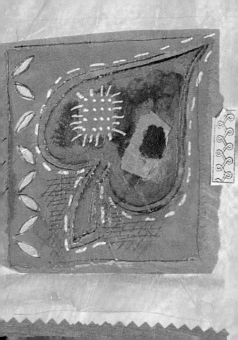

The only way
to have a
friend
is to be one.

RALPH WALDO EMERSON

Show me a friend
who will weep
with me; those
who will laugh
with me I can
find myself.

YUGOSLAVIAN PROVERB

♥

# A faithful friend is the medicine of life.

FROM THE OLD TESTAMENT
BOOK OF ECCLESIASTES

I never set out to *make* a best friend; you can't manufacture that. But one day I looked at the people in my life – and she was already there: the truest friend one could ever hope to find.

FRANCES GRANT

Lord, deliver me from the plastic Jesus, the stone Buddha, and the pious voices. Open me to my neighbour's touch, and the sounds of Life, in all its forms.

K. BRADFORD BROWN

I rang up my friend to complain about my problems, and then she told me hers. It helped both of us.

COLETTE MAYNARD

Don't go in front of me,
I may not follow.
Don't go behind me,
I may not lead.
Just go beside
me, and be my
friend.

ALBERT CAMUS

It's only when you've got
rid of all the *yah-yah* bits
of your life, the need to
shout, to bang your fist,
that you can slip into
the quietness, and realize
– God is your friend,
walking beside you.

DOUGLAS GIFFORD

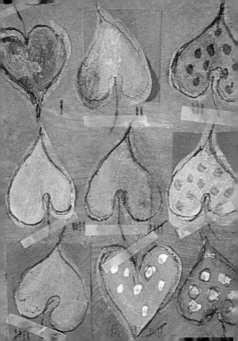